First Edition
Genuine Autographed Collectible

_____

Do you want me to sign it in ink or in lipstick?

The Philosophy of Love

Gift Card

Date:

To:

From:

Message:

Self-Help, Relationships, Philosophy of Love, Spirituality, Sharon Esther Lampert

If You Practice SELF-LOVE You Will Never Spend a Day in Therapy - The Philosophy of Love

©2025 First Edition by Sharon Esther Lampert. All Rights Reserved.
No part of this book may be used or reproduced in any manner whatsoever without written permission except in the case of brief quotations embodied in critical articles and reviews.
No part of this book may be used or reproduced in any manner for the purpose of training artificial intelligence technologies or systems. In accordance with Article 4(3) of the Digital Single Market Directive 2019/790, (KADIMAH PRESS) expressly reserves this work from the text and data mining exception.

KADIMAH PRESS
Gifts of Genius

Books may be purchased for education, business, or sales promotional use.
ISBN Hardcover: 979-8-3481-6157-6
ISBN Paperback: 979-8-3481-6160-6
ISBN e-book: 979-8-3481-6161-3
Library of Congress Catalog Card Number: 2024926832

FAN MAIL:
SharonEstherLampert.com
FANS@SharonEstherLampert.com

Cover and Interior Book Design: Creative Genius Sharon Esther Lampert
Editor: Dave Segal

Palm Beach Book Publisher, Phone: 917-767-5843
Sharon@PalmBeachBookPublisher.com
To Order Book:
Ingram, 1 Ingram Blvd. La Vergne, TN 37086-3629
Phone: 615-793-5000
Fax orders: 615-287-6990

First Edition

Manufactured in the United States of America

Age 9
THE QUEEN HAS ARRIVED!
My daughter is a poet, philosopher, and teacher. She is the Princess & Pea! BEAUTY & BRAINS!
LOVE & XOXO
MOMMY

WORLD FAMOUS POEM

TRUE LOVE

True Love Is Unconditional
True Love Is Found in the Deed
True Love Is Found in the We
True Love Joins the Heart
Mind, and Body as One

Sharon Esther Lampert

Dedication

MOMMY
LOVE OF MY LIFETIME

What Do Books Do?
BOOKS ARE POWERFUL

Books Educate!
Books Enlighten!
Books Empower!
Books Emancipate!
Books Entertain!
Books Spring Eternal!
Books Drive Exploration!
Books Spark Evolution!
Books Ignite Revolution!

Sharon Esther Lampert

The Philosophy of Love

If You Practice **SELF-LOVE** You Will Never Spend a Day in Therapy

KADIMAH PRESS
Gifts of Genius

Table of Contents

What Is Love?

What Is Self-Love?

Two Kinds of Love: Me & We

Two Kinds of Self-Love: True Love Is Self-Love & Bonus Love

Two Kinds of Relationships:
1% Unconditional True Love — True Love Lottery Ticket
99.9% Conditional Transactional Love — Expiration Date

Reason, Season or Lifetime — Maya Angelou

What Plan Are You On?

Two Kinds of Partners: Prospects or Projects?

Laws of Inextricability: Love & Hate

Metamorphosis: Grow Together or Grow Apart

Lessons Learned

WORLD FAMOUS QUOTE

What Is Love?

You Don't Find Love
You Create Love

Sharon Esther Lampert

Love Is a Practice

Q: What Does Daily SELF-LOVE Look Like?
Did You Put Some Love Into It?
Self-Care of Your Mind, Body, and Spirit

1. Love Yourself First
2. Eat Whole Foods
3. Exercise Regularly
4. Build Brain Power
5. Practice Inner Peace
6. Regular Bedtime

There Is No Such Thing As Too Much Love!

Sharon Esther Lampert

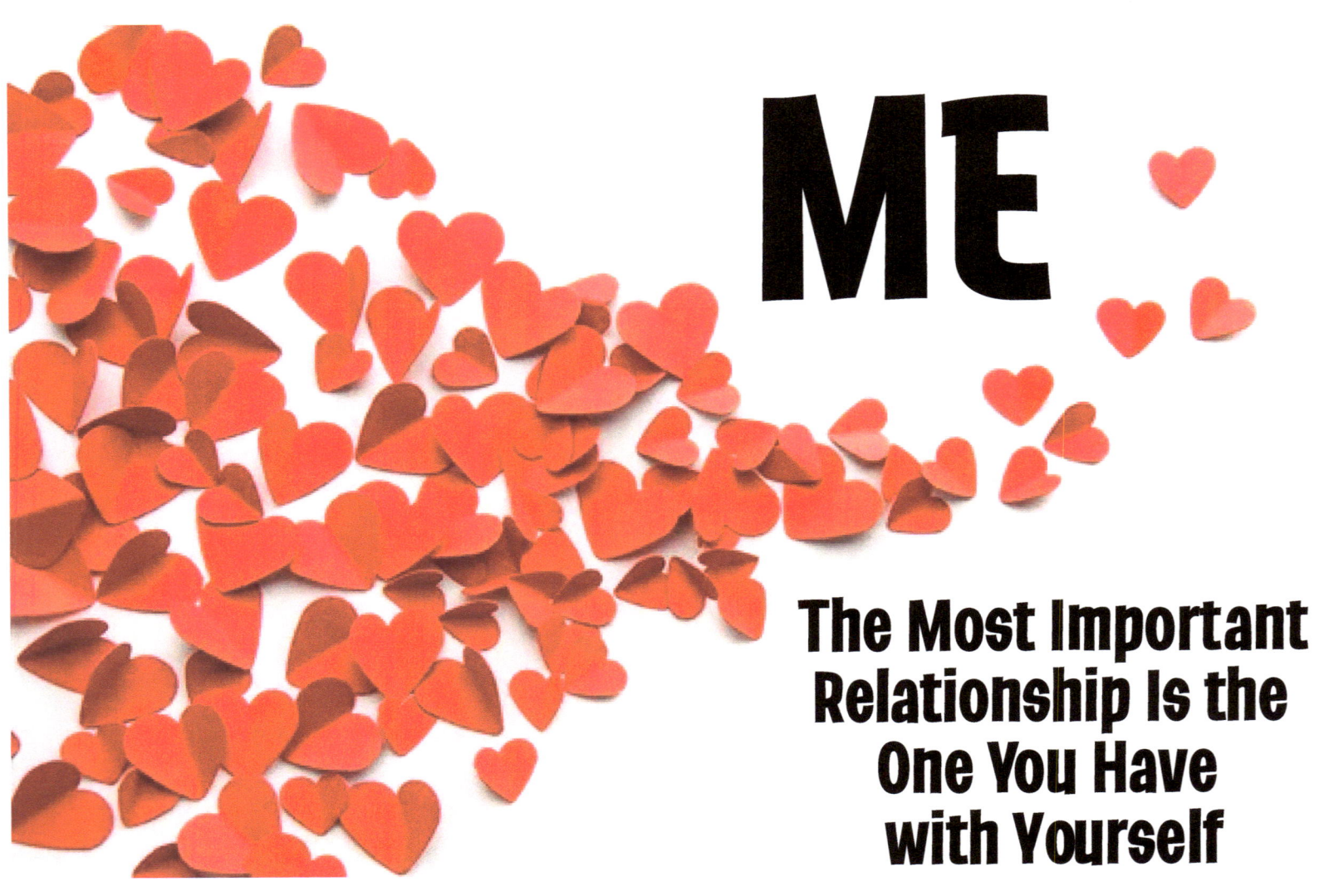

"Love each other for what you are; forgive each other for what you ain't!"
— unknown

WE

You Can Never Know Another Person

You Will Marry a Stranger
You Will Have Sex with a Stranger
You Will Have Children With a Stranger
You Will Divorce a Stranger

— Philosopher Queen Sharon Esther Lampert

"When someone shows you who they are, believe them the first time." — Maya Angelou

WE

Most People Do Not Have Enough Love Inside of Themselves for Themselves — Let Alone to Love You

99.9% of Relationships Are Accidental Occurrences: Lucky? Unlucky? Lucky & Unlucky?

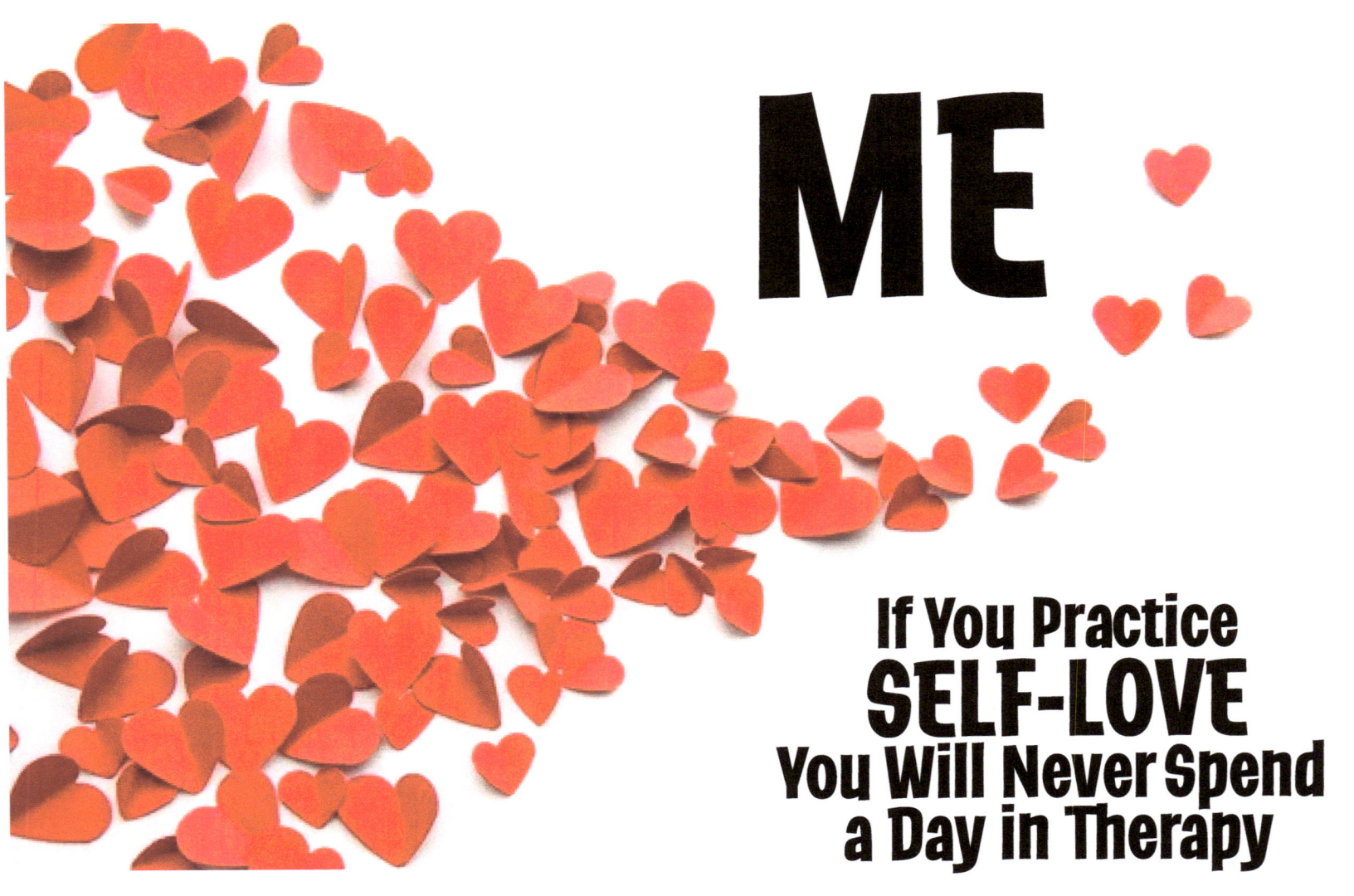

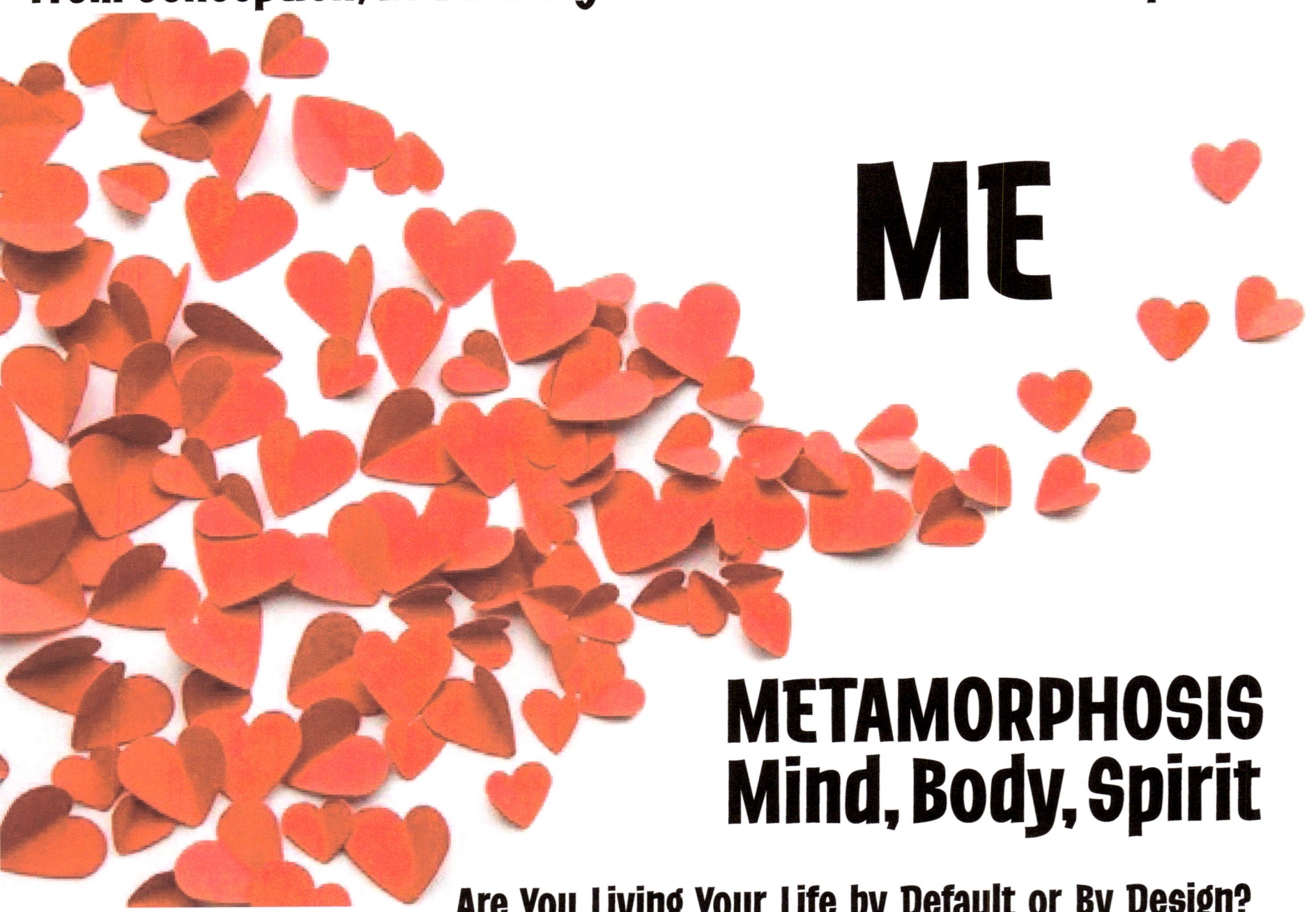

WORLD FAMOUS QUOTE

People Come into Your Life for a Reason, a Season, or a Lifetime

Maya Angelou

99.% of People for a Reason

True Unconditional Love Is Real But Rare!
True Love Burns Eternal

Like Winning a Lottery Ticket
Everyone Buys a Lottery Ticket
But Only One Person Wins at True Love

Happily Married Couples Married Their Best Friends

The Loss of True Love Is Excruciating; Time Does Not Heal a Broken Heart

— Philosopher Queen Sharon Esther Lampert

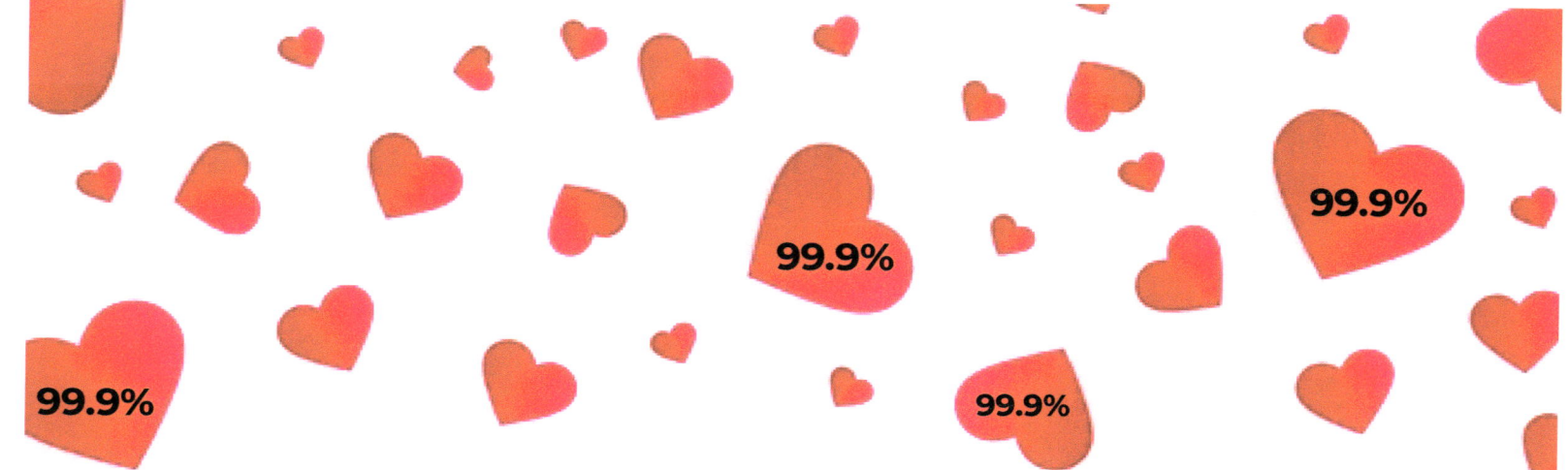

99.9 % of Love Is CONDITIONAL TRANSACTIONAL LOVE

— Love Only What They Want From You —
There Is an Expiration Date
Ghosting, Break-Up, Infidelity, Divorce

"50% of People are Trying to Get Into a Relationship, and the other 50% of People are Trying to Get Out of a Relationship."
— Philosopher Queen Sharon Esther Lampert

Our World Is Organized by Laws of Inextricability

Q. Why is the person you love and married the same person you hate and divorced?

LAWS of INEXTRICABILITY

All People Help You with Their Strengths and Hurt You with Their Weaknesses

Love and Hate Are Inextricabily Linked

99.9% of Relationships Are Love-Hate Relationships

DYSFUNCTIONAL DOMESTIC DRAMA

Q: What PLAN Are You On?

1. Casual Sex?
2. Extra-Marietal Casual Sex?
3. Friends with Benefits?
4. Dating?
5. Boyfriend/Girlfriend?
6. Significant Other?
7. Sexting Plan?
8. Life Partner?
9. Family Plan?
10. Other?

Ask This Simple Question to Save Yourself from Wasting Time with the Wrong Partner

Two Kinds of Partners: Prospects or Projects?

Broken World of Broken People
Generational Drama & Trauma
5 Out of 5 People Have
Mental Health Distress
1 Out of 5 People Have an
Undiagnosed Mental Illness

Projects Need a Full Time
PSYCHIATRIST
NOT A PARTNER

"Good People Nothing Is a Problem; Bad People Everything Is a Problem"
— Philosopher Queen Sharon Esther Lampert

WORLD FAMOUS POEM

IMPOSSIBLE

It is **IMPOSSIBLE** to breathe in air,
Without breathing in toxic pollutants.

It is **IMPOSSIBLE** to ingest nutritious food,
Without ingesting chemicals and preservatives.

It is **IMPOSSIBLE** to have a loving relationship,
Without bumping into a loved one's problems.

And it is **IMPOSSIBLE** not to **BREATHE**, **EAT**, and **LOVE**.

Sharon Esther Lampert

The Philosophy of Love: 14 Lessons Learned

1. **You Don't Find Love, You Create Love**
   Love Is a Daily Practice
   Practice: Kindness, Respect, Empathy, and Trust

2. Two Kinds of Love: **ME** & **WE**

3. Two Kinds of Self-Love: **Self-Love** & Bonus Love

4. ME: **SELF LOVE IS TRUE LOVE**

5. ME: SELF LOVE IS NOT SELFISH

6. WE: You Can Never Know Another Person

7. WE: Love From Outside Yourself Is **BONUS LOVE**

8. Two Kinds of Love: **Unconditional True Love** & Conditional Transactional Love
   1%   Unconditional True Love - Real But Rare!
   99%   Conditional Transactional Love - Only Love What They Want From You!

9. Happily Married Couples Married Their **BEST FRIENDS**

10. Ask the Simple Question: **What Plan Are You On?**

11. Prospects or Projects?

12. PHYSICS: Our World Is Organized By **LAWS OF INEXTRICABILITY: LOVE & HATE**
    99.9 % of All Relationships Are Love-Hate Relationships
    All People Help You with Their Strengths and Hurt You with Their Weaknesses

13. BIOLOGY: From Conception to Death, We Undergo the Process of **METAMORPHOSIS**
    You Will Grow Together or Grow Apart

14. LUCK: Are you lucky? Are you unlucky? Are you lucky and unlucky?
    99.9% of Relationships Are Accidental Occurrences

GENIUS: THE GIFT OF DIVINE REVELATION

MY BOOKS WRITE THEMSELVES

I Am Mortal.
My Books Are Immortal.
Please Handle My Books Gently.
My Books Are My Remains.

This book was written in one day
Part 1. Birth of Idea - December 15, 2024
Part 2. Format Book — December 16 2024
Part 3. Publish — December 17, 2024

Also By The Genius

1. CUPID — Written in Letter C
2. LOVE YOU MORE THAN YESTERDAY: 14 Relationship Strategies for Happily Ever After
3. SEX ON A PLATE: FOOD AS FOREPLAY, THE COOKBOOK OF EVERLASTING LOVE

Sharon Esther Lampert
SEE THE WORLD THROUGH THE EYES OF A CREATIVE GENIUS
Poet, Philosopher, Prophet, Peacemaker, Paladin of Education, Princess, Prodigy

FANS@SharonEstherLampert.com

www.ingramcontent.com/pod-product-compliance
Lightning Source LLC
LaVergne TN
LVHW071734060526
838201LV00039B/407